2012

THE ENDING OF THE WILLIE LYNCH LETTER

Let's Renovate!

by

Leander Brown a.k.a. "Phenomenal Le"

DORRANCE PUBLISHING CO., INC.
PITTSBURGH, PENNSYLVANIA 15222

Dorrance Publishing Co., Inc.
701 Smithfield Street
Pittsburgh, PA 15222
Visit our website at *www.dorrancebookstore.com*

ISBN: 978-1-4809-0229-9
eISBN: 978-1-4809-0522-1

CONTENTS

INTRODUCTION

I wrote this piece to enlighten the minds of people in the world, especially blacks/African-Americans, about the negative psychological effects of the Willie Lynch Letter. This malicious labyrinth has impacted many lives, causing ignorance, broken homes, disrespectfulness, and poor health throughout the nation. I'm concentrating more on aiding blacks/African-Americans because this ethnic group statistically leads America in negative aspects of life, such as heart disease, poverty, broken homes, incarcerations, lack of education, etc.— and the fact that this system was directed toward African-Americans. Although all cultures and nationalities suffer from such downfalls because of such a melting pot society we live in, any man, woman, or child is capable of falling victim to Lynch's negative behavioral application. Mankind, as a whole, needs an improvement. If you've neither read nor heard of the written phenomenon called the Willie Lynch Letter: The Making of a Slave, go and read that letter first so you would be able to read this startling letter as a prerequisite in order to have a better understanding of how this matrix of ignorance has enslaved the mind, body, and soul of individuals for centuries.

Willie Lynch was a manipulative man from Great Britain who owned slaves in the West Indies. Most people may recognize him by the act of his sinister last name, *lynching*. In 1712, Lynch traveled to the colony of Virginia and lectured the slave owners (whites/Caucasians) there on how to better control their slaves by using the teaching of negativity such as doubt, jealousy, and terror. The younger generation is more familiar with these acts as "hating." His system was intended to last for a minimum of 300 years, making the year 2012 the ending for this uncivilized bondage that has been plaguing our society. Now, would you agree that this is strikingly ironic?

The Lynch theory has been implemented for so long that it created an environment of self-destruction by clouding the conscious and subconscious minds, fueling one's natural way of thinking (striving for greatness) with negativity and making it the prime thinker, simply wasting time and hurting yourself and your environment in the process. This system forces you to oppress yourself by making you concentrate on the least important and veering one from the important things of life, like focusing on your health and thinking positively. Your life is birthed from the mind first. When you initially think toward the good of existence and continue down that path, there is no other choice but good to be birthed through the mind, body, and soul. Ever heard of the old cliché of giving a person a rope and watch him hang himself? Well, Lynch's letter is a replica of the cliché.

It quickly became an epidemic, an intangible oppression that allows the soul of the oppressed to become his or her own enemy. It's bad enough that the African slaves were stripped of their heritage, but being forced to learn negativity leaves a culture with a deteriorating character. This promotion of genocide must stop before we, as mankind, ultimately destroy our planet. This change takes work; it's not an overnight success tactic that will repair hundreds of years of turmoil. It will be a process to get back on a more ethical path of enlightenment for the men, women, and children within the black/African-American communities. This process must start with attaining and maintaining good health. Focusing on your health and strengthening your mental and physical powers will indeed create a more supreme individual, thus birthing an everlasting effect of promoting euphoria, and destroying evil.

Throughout this piece, I will be giving realistic scenarios from my own past experiences and from other individuals who I have witnessed struggling with human relations and interactions. These examples I give will show a comparison with today's issues and Lynch's letter of intent to bring forth a better understanding on this message that I attempt to convey. I was raised in an inner city and lived in others; I've lived in multicultural communities as well, so I know that the effects of Lynch's letter do exist.

I know with the creation of this written phenomenon, I've sparked some controversy that everyone will not agree on and may offend some people in the world. Hey, I'll take all the criticism and stones thrown at me and carry them on my shoulders so that my dreams of increasing the ratio of the elite transpire over into reality.

My intention is to bring awareness to the world on how the implementation of this letter has negatively affected the conduct of individuals by weakening the mind, causing poor human interactions and a slave mentality to those who fall subject to Lynch's influences. I'm not pointing the finger at any particular race or person; I'm pointing the finger at the issue at hand and giving a solution for the issue. My goal is to help cultivate the mind and soul of mankind by altering Lynch's system of corruption, so that blacks/African-Americans regain control over their lives for a more harmonious, balanced, and peaceful existence. Ambition for life will be exalted beyond its pinnacle. It's a world full of people who have the qualities and capabilities of Ray Lewis, Shawn Carter (Jay Z), Michael Jordan, Picasso, Barrack and Michelle Obama, Oprah, Michael Jackson, and many others who house that inner substance of greatness—universal energy. Revolutionize your thinking process through the incorporation of love, the essence of our natural being. The year 2012 doesn't mark the end of the world; it marks the ending of a ludicrous process that needs attention in order to restore civilization throughout the world.

LYNCH'S SPEECH ANALYSIS

On December 25, 1712, Willie Lynch was invited to the Colony of Virginia to deliver a speech among the slave owners because they felt that they were losing control of their slaves on the plantations. Basically, the slaves were rebelling against the owners by fighting for and running away to freedom. This defiance left the plantation in peril with neglected vegetation, arsons, and deaths of farm animals. Just think—you were captured and taken to an unknown land, around strangers of a different language and culture, and was forced to work every day from sunup until sundown in the worst of conditions, along with being brutally beaten and fed scraps. I'm quite sure anyone wouldn't like it and would try to escape. But Lynch had the answers to keep the slaves in check. He studied human behavior with his own slaves in the West Indies in order to understand how to manipulate them into being obedient to his tyrannical beliefs. His method of controlling the slaves was by replacing their natural being of strength and vitality with the installation of fear in their minds and hearts, and persuasion of being distrustful and envious of one another. Lynch knew that by defying the laws of nature within the slaves, the majority of the slaves would struggle with being outspoken for justice, creativity, courage, health, targeting all the aspects of life that should come first, which builds a stronger, intelligent you. Mankind was created to live prosperously, harmoniously, and with great integrity within our environment. It doesn't matter if you are religious or not; the main objective of life is to work hard at eliminating and reducing pain, and cultivating love for yourself and your surroundings—creating and attracting a divine existence. Author Rhonda Byrne noted that, "When you feel bad, you are on the frequency of drawing more bad things. When you feel good, you are powerfully attracting more good things to you" (page 43, paragraph 5).

I'm quite sure no one wants to go throughout life with growing aches and pains, stress, and poor human relations. This may make a person lazy, ill mannered, and quick to give up when things get overwhelming. Why? It is because of the years an individual spent tormenting his natural essence. When this happens, the energy of your mind and body weakens and may not be strong enough to handle overwhelming situations. Or know how to, for that matter. Joy and pain will always exist, but you want your time-spent ratio to be higher on the joy side of things, to a point that pain feels nonexistent.

For instance, I myself have suffered from different effects of the Willie Lynch Letter, like constantly worrying about bills or catching myself wasting time. But the Willie Lynch Letter can never destroy your essence. There is always a light in the mist of darkness that shines and proliferate when you take heed of how your decision making affect your well-being, presently and futuristically. There had also been a time when I would get easily upset and take it out on someone or something that did not have anything to do with why I was upset. All that does is generate a domino effect of negative energy. For example, one may get upset with his or her job, then come home and yell at his or her kids, pets, or someone close to him or her. Instead of trying to find the root of your bitterness and fixing it, you might stuff a candy bar down your throat or chug down a soda, trying to find relief in food. The issue will still be there, getting worst, along with your health.

There have been many different analyses revealing that African-Americans lead the nation in poor health. Dr. Monika Stafford from the University of Alabama at Birmingham set out a team of researchers to conduct a four-year study on African-Americans and white Americans, in which none of the volunteers has had any problems with heart disease. According to a recent article hosted by MedlinePlus, Genevra Pittman reported that, "Every year during the study, 4 in 1,000 black men died from heart disease, on average, compared to 1.9 white men, the researchers found. Among women, 2 in 1,000 blacks died of heart disease each year, compared to 1 in 1,000 whites" (page1, paragraph 7). The study only show how many deaths occurred, not how many people who are living with health issues such as diabetes, high blood pressure, high cholesterol, etc. This all falls back to the Willie Lynch Letter, which consists of psychologically forcing people to make poor choices concerning ones' health, and other important aspects of life. Poor choices then trickles down to the environment you influence: family, friends, media, and all things of nature are watered down.

Willie Lynch used three main concepts to implement his tyrannical philosophy: envy, distrust, and fear. He also used such differences of age, gender, magnitude, and complexion to help master his system. For example, Lynch forced negative interactions between the slaves, and vice versa of, such as elder

2

male slaves against younger male slaves, the darker skin slaves against lighter skin slaves, and the male against the female. He also proposed that all white people distrust all blacks, and that the blacks should only trust, adore, and admire white people.

Envy, Distrust, Fear

Envy, distrust, and fear are the center point from which the negative interactions are birth. A person should never, under any circumstances, become bitter, jealous, hateful, or against oneself or any other individual. This is a negative creation. Avoid letting these come to your mind. Your initial and continual thought should never produce it. But if it does, fix it by getting it out of your thoughts so that negative results do not occur. A person may be bitter about his appearance. Either you can try to fix your appearance to your liking or find some qualities about your appearance that you like, and that makes you different in a positive way. Example, a woman may feel bitter about her hairstyle. Just change your hairstyle or find your own reason to like it and not care about what others think about it. If what you think about it creates satisfaction and serenity within yourself, then that's all that matters. Only have an open ear to others' comments that adds to your satisfaction and serenity, because if someone thinks or makes a negative comment about your hair, then that person is suffering from the Willie Lynch Letter. You have to think to yourself, *This person just made an initial, irrelevant, negative comment about my hair; she is trying to bring misery to me by influencing my thinking process about my own hair that I love, and that God loves unconditionally.* You must not let what you hear or see leave a negative effect on you that will continue to grow. The average person would think about that negative comment that may produce self-doubt, or he or she may bring up that negative comment later on in a conversation, fueling the WLL. Turn it around into something positive. If you do not try to turn something negative as such into something positive, that's when distrust and fear follows. Then, you start to distrust the person who made the comment. You start to distrust your own judgment, which morphs into you becoming more vulnerable to negativity.

Now fear just put the icing on the cake. Fear makes a person fall subject to negativity and produces an ongoing effect unless scrutinized or addressed, and creating positive processes to make the best of it. Now, you fear everything, including yourself; fear that you can't do or say a positive thing in a diverse way; fear of what others may think or say; and fear of risk, change, acceptance, emotional response, confrontation—to ask questions, truth, fear itself. You carry that burden around with you 24/7. Why? Just let it go and get to the bottom of your fear. Ask yourself, what I can do to make myself happy? How can I spend my time doing something positive? Think about it, see yourself doing it, gather supporters, and do it. Create a positive atmosphere because fear only promotes stress and strain on mankind. And this depression stems from one comment of an infinity amount that you allow to change your thinking process from thinking highly. Living a healthy lifestyle promotes positive thinking and becomes a force field against any negative thought or energy that tries to enter your mind, body, and soul.

Elder versus Younger

Now let's take a look at some of these scenarios and how it relates to the world we live in today. The elder African-American male versus the younger African-American male is a conflict that you hear or/and see on a daily basis in America. The elder are usually against the younger because they think that the younger generation is out of control as far as their behavior, style, choice of music, etc. are concerned.

In some instances, some of the younger males may have screwed-up attitudes and have no respect for life, but not all are like that. Remember, everything that exists has an opposite, so there are some respectful younger African-American males. It would be wrong to say, "I can't be around the younger crowd. They're too wild and disrespectful." I've heard it numerous times. This way of thinking only creates separation and fuels the Willie Lynch Letter effect. The main reason why some of the younger African-Americans are a little more out of control is because of the elder African-American generation not spending time to educate and influence them to become civilized young men and women from the beginning, forcing immaturity to find its own way of direction. Hormone levels are already all over the place in developing young kids; the nation needs more African-American men and women to lead and give the younger generation a more serene sense of direction. The simplest of actions can help uplift the mind, body, and soul. There have been times when I was standing in line behind some kids at a convenient store. The clerk ringed up the kids juice, chips, etc. Sadly, the kids were short or money. The clerk told the kids that they can't have it and started to put the items back. I told the clerk to put the remaining balance on my bill. The kids' face brightened with joy and they thanked me. You see, moments like this one goes a long way. I stepped up and created a change for the better without having to be the children's guardian. This positive happening promotes good karma and universal energy connecting with the law of attraction. I encourage the elder generation to step up and guide the young men, women, and children of today's society. Get involved in the world of recreational arts, such as martial arts, dance, music, writing, acting, sports, physical fitness, creative invention, culinary arts, and many other activities that automatically deter mankind away from any hardships of life and more toward a rapturous well-being.

If you're going to be bold enough to criticize, be bold enough to manifest solutions for your criticism.

Younger versus Elder

Now, with the younger generation not wanting to connect with the older generation, it is usually because the younger generation believes that the older ones do not have knowledge, wisdom, or understanding about the present and future, only the past. But what the younger generation fails to understand is that their present and future are the elder's past. This is where experience comes into play. The elder generation may have gone through and/or witnessed experiences that the younger generation is going through or may be heading. Younger generation, don't get all frustrated when an elder gives you advice because frustration is futile. I'm quite sure that any elder's idea is for your best interest. Sometimes, advice could be vague to a developing mind, so don't be afraid to ask questions to understand the who, what, when, where, why, and how of the situation at hand. I'm not telling you to look up to any and every elder you encounter. Advice and help should be taken from a sound individual who makes positive, valid points and expresses it through his or her character and actions. I always say you can learn at least two things from a person: what to do and what not to do.

Dark Skin versus Light skin

I say that we all should be able to agree that skin color shouldn't matter when dealing with a person's character and actions. There's no comparison between the two. Back during the days of slavery, the slave owners would separate the light-skinned from the dark-skinned slaves by allowing the light-skinned slaves to work within the slave owner's household, while the dark-skinned slaves worked in the fields and lived outside the household in some of the worst conditions imaginable. The WLL caused the dark-skinned slaves to dislike the light-skinned slaves because they lived in the house with the owners and received better treatment. It also created assumption that the light-skinned slaves were better that the darker ones. I have personally seen this scenario myself. I've met darker-skinned African-Americans say that light-skinned African-Americans act conceitedly, stuck up, and quick to tell your business. That causes a person to become prejudiced. Just because you have met some light-skinned African-Americans who think and act that way, it doesn't mean that all light-skinned people are that way. The ones you met are suffering from this aspect of the WLL effect, and you are, too, because you initially prejudge them. Thinking that way creates a smoke screen from the truth, considering a person's character and actions. Now this could possibly allow someone with darker skin to treat you more badly than the light-skinned person that you assumed would treat you badly. That's one hell of a rhetorical device that is self-fueling against you.

Light skin versus Dark skin

Now, on the other side of things, the light-skinned slaves were forced to believe that they were better than the darker slaves because the lighter-skinned slaves were given better living conditions and treatment. If you are a light-skinned individual who thinks you are better than anyone who is darker than you, you're only prejudging yourself before getting to know the other person. Somewhere in the world, there is someone who is better than you in particular areas of your life, because no one is perfect in all they do. Someone has to fill that void of imperfection. So why even let that thought enter your thinking process? All that does is alienate yourself from people who may bring good to your life. These days, we live in a diverse, melting pot society, and we all want good and great things for ourselves. We just have to do better as a whole, and it starts with you. Let go of being racist, prejudiced, and not giving people a chance because of their skin.

Female versus Male, and Vice Versa

We all need one another, especially when it comes to women and men. You can't be complete without the balance of both in your life in its physical and mental form. The best way to become balanced is to come together and learn from one another, because a woman can think, say, and do things a man possibly couldn't, and vice versa. Both women and men shouldn't get involved with one another if one or the other is non-value added. Bring something to the table other than sex and beauty. Show that balance of masculinity and femininity in the mind, body, and soul.

If you are a man who possesses the masculinity traits of unyielding, aggressiveness, and knowledge, learn some feminine aspects of life, such as patience, receptiveness, and wisdom. This teaches you how to find peace within yourself, and to interact with the opposite sex. Stop being fearful and work toward understanding and correcting issues. Don't be quick to give up or fly off at the handle, which makes matters worst. Cases of domestic violence and broken homes will statistically diminish when we focus on these aspects of life. Children will grow up with both parents involved in their lives, so they won't grow up aiding to the negative statistics of this nation, this world. Conduct some research in the US Census Bureau; numbers don't lie. African-Americans lead in categories of being unsuccessful as far as average income, incarcerations, broken homes, etc. Making a change in these numbers all starts with you! Don't just talk about it; be about it as well.

Blacks Only Trusting Whites, Whites Not Trusting Blacks

The WLL system also enforced the black population to only trust the white population. This is just another cover up to distract the mind from the truth of trusting peoples' character and actions. The system designed a redundancy of encountering discomfort and pain. The blacks, during the era of slavery, would trust the white slave owners and overseers' words. The blacks were tricked into believing that they needed and only needed to depend on the whites. This created a repeating cycle of lies and entrapment of freedom, hope, faith, overall strength, and bliss. This aspect of the WLL created an atmosphere of a lot of African-Americans distrustful of their own kind, or any other race that is not white, which is wrong.

How can you go throughout life not trusting your own brother or sister, relative, your neighbor? And the whites were taught that they should not trust any of the blacks within the colonies. What all these do is to minimize the diversity of your thinking process and create fear and ignorance. Why? All because of someone's skin? Totally absurd! I never knew that skin shade could hurt someone; only the negative energy one produces and expresses through his actions could. I've met people from all races, including mix races, and met some of the most divine beings ever. And I am blessed to be able to learn and enjoy from a conglomeration of people to help me become a more efficient and divine individual. Being open minded unlocks an infinite amount of opportunities. Building on universal power is another way of snapping the WLL effect.

LET'S CIVILIZE A SLAVE

The Willie Lynch Letter had so much success because he encouraged the slave owners to analyze human nature so that they will know how to control the slaves. In human nature, when we discover pain, most of us try to find a way to bring joy to our lives and every aspect of it. And to do so, we must be able to follow a process to get back to the state of mind that brings us peace. Willie Lynch emptied out the positive aspects in the blacks and replaced it with negative aspects, and monitored their behavior and actions. By doing so, the system allowed the slave owners to simulate a chess game. By knowing what tactics the blacks would take to free their minds, bodies, and souls, the slave owners would cut off all possibilities of gaining their freedom by introducing pain, uncivilized living, and death on all levels. This takes away from your natural state of living or knowing how to live, leaving one lost, confused, and operated by controlled negativity. Lynch incorporated the same basic doctrines on the slaves, one used to break down a horse.

He used the power of a thing for its own usage without civilized resistance. So the main way to reverse this principle is to get back to the basics. People need to work toward their natural state of being in order to gain freedom of mind, body, and soul. Number one on your to-do list should be "taking care of yourself." If a person cannot take care of himself, how could he care for his environment? In this day and age, we have seen a change in society, of people wanting to live healthier lives. The major thing is that most of us do not know how to take care of ourselves, or get distracted from doing so. It starts with the mind, knowing how to take care of yourself, implementing the research of unbreakable consistency of gaining strength, and then reaping the introverted and extroverted benefits of universal power. Research, research, and more research for information are required before putting a process of healthy living into your life in order to ensure an efficient lifestyle. We as a people have to commit ourselves to a lifestyle change. To break down this process even further, we need to commit the majority of our time throughout the day focusing on our strength and learning from our weaknesses. We must capitalize on our opportunities to present a change for the better. My personal basic step, which I used for myself and found to be very helpful, is to rid the mind of any fear or doubt. Stop making excuses of not having time to do this or that, or you are scared to workout because of the temporary soreness it brings to your muscles. I even hear people say, "It costs too much to eat healthy." Saying statements like these gives yourself an out, a grey area of riding the fence instead of hopping off onto the positive side of finding an efficient way of eating healthier meals and time management.

You have to reverse this thinking process. You have to say to yourself, "I will make time for a healthy living. I am not afraid of pain and will do everything in my power to dwindle it. I will use my mind to find an efficient way of getting vital nutrients into my mind, body, and soul without spending a lot of money. I will be consistent in doing so no matter what anyone says or think about my transformation because I know the positive outcome it brings to me and my environment." Remember, you have to have an open mind in incorporating different strategies from different cultures that best fit you. Now, once you have that thinking process embedded into the mind, you have to feed it by taking care of your body. Start with a complete body cleansing system. You must continue to rid yourself of any toxins that will make you feel sluggish and weak in any way. For example, if someone were to plant a garden, you wouldn't want plant seeds on a land filled with broken bottles and cigarette butts, would you? Of course not. The same principles apply to taking care of you. Get rid of the corrosion then plant the seed of life and continue to monitor it for positive gain. Most Americans are filled with toxins from unhealthy eating and other bad habits that take away from seeing the full potential of our growth. Now, you have to commit to a routine of self-building through the arts of various fitness regimes, meditation, yoga, etc. Then get involve with recreational events such as sports, music, art institutes, martial arts, humanitarian deeds, things of that nature that challenge you mentally, physically, and emotionally. No one is perfect, but you can at least show some effort of becoming strong and healthy for yourself and your family. Learn how to maintain your fabulous transformation so that, in time, the floodgate of blessings will open to you. I am an essence connecter and holistic healer so I know firsthand the effects of positive transformation. Also, make it your business to see a doctor to stay updated with your health status.

If you can't afford health care, go to your local library and open a book, or use their computers and learn how to live healthier. Once you have the pattern of healthy living, share the knowledge you gained with your love ones.

I'm simply providing basic notifications that need attention in today's society. My goal is to reduce pain, struggles, and suffering for mankind, especially the African-American communities.

CARDINAL PRINCIPLES OF CIVILIZING A MAN

This portion of the WLL explains how the breaking process worked on the black male slaves during it's time, which became metamorphic for 300 years. Lynch started with the mind because the mind gives birth to the reaction of the body. A mental breakdown results in a physical breakdown as well; that way, the slave owners were able to control the slaves for economic growth. So to reverse this process, one must be able to resist within the mind no matter how down and out you may think you're experiencing. You must have resistance to pain, injustice, fear, or any aspect of life that brings and births negativity, because negativity holds no value; if not, one will embrace and accept pain as a natural state of being. I see and hear this occurrence throughout society today. Sometimes, men, we get broken down to a point of feeling like there is no hope, no routes to take on the road to peace and happiness within our lives. Then we begin to wonder, will we ever reach peace, happiness, heaven? The answer is simply yes. You must say to yourself, "I will and I am doing what is necessary and relevant to sustain life and support God, or the power that be." Strive to stay away from thoughts of words like "I might," "I was," "It's possible." They only leave room for your thinking process to slip to a slave mentality of fear, with usage of words like "I can't," "I won't," "I didn't."

Men, you must use your mind for the grace of good in order to strengthen your essence, the true substance of life. Do not accept nor run away from pain, injustice, or fear. Men, we must destroy pain, injustice, and fear. Educate the mind on how to bring good in your life. Learn, learn, learn, and stop being afraid of failing, because the opposite of failing is success, resurrection of the mind. No excuses for why you can't attain enlightenment. Laziness in the mind is really what is holding people back. And to gain that enlightenment, you have to take care of yourself. The first cardinal principle of civilization is to make sure you are getting proper nutrition daily, and that you are committing to some sort of strengthening and conditioning activities for the mind and body that will allow your soul to shine. Taking care of your health eliminates mental, physical, and spiritual fatigue. It starts with the men first. We influence our surroundings. We were born to take on a leadership role to sustain life. Then share your intelligence within the household. Teach our families how to eat and live healthier, and stand your ground on it. Learn about laws, finances, management, technology, communication, art, and subjects that help build an efficient household. Strong health helps you to handle stress and hardships that come into your life. Have the mental and physical discipline to deflect pain, or turn it into something positive as quickly as possible. I guarantee that the consistency of these principles will turn your life around for the better. With doing so, the oppressor cannot pinpoint your actions and stop your growth because the oppressor's sinister predictions are destroyed by reversing the psychological chess game that has been lingering around for years. Booby traps are set up all around us; destroy them or go around them. Men, especially African-American men, flip the "light" switch on in your minds and manifest your divine essence!

THE BUILDING PROCESS OF THE WOMAN

The building process of the woman is very important because she is Mother Nature and is the birthplace of intelligence and strength. The things you see, hear, communicate, experience, and around with influence the development of yourself, your offspring, and your household. Doing so creates a redundant cycle and can be passed down to her offspring during pregnancy and/or after the child is born. Again, I must stress the importance of health within the human body in order for the essence of nature to continue to flourish. Women, you all have to get it together. You can't be roaming the Earth every day absorbing and housing negativity, or associating yourself around people, places, or things that bring you down. If you are not receiving the proper nutrients into your body year after year, then your offspring will have a hard time receiving proper nutrition because the parent(s) have the authority over the child. Too many children are born into this world with birth defects and many other potential health risks because of the women not taking care of themselves efficiently. No one knows if it's possible to eliminate birth defects, mentally or physically, but I know that the number of birth defects can be reduced abundantly.

Single or not, get involve with physical fitness and art. Spend the majority of your time doing things that make you stronger inside and out, rather than spending the majority of your time that is non-value added. Just stop and ask yourself, "Is my decision making helping my kid(s) and me, and creating a strong and stable home? If not, you will attract stressful and non-value added things into your life. When that happens, you point the finger at everyone else but yourself when, in reality, you can't point a finger without having three fingers pointing back at you.

Correct your own actions. Rather you know it or not, your child see, hear, communicate, and try to act out everything he or she witnesses from you. So what do you want while you are here on Earth? Creating a life cycle of hard times for you and your family, or a life of greatness? All you have to do is just stand up and do it! Don't just talk about it, be about it! Back your words up with sound actions. No need to complain about how your appearance looks, how men aren't worth anything, your health. Either fix it by creating and living a cycle of executing the unwanted or suffer. Scrutinize every person, place, or thing you encounter or haven't encountered yet. Either it will help my family and me or hurt it; then figure out how. Accept only grand expectations for yourself, and for/from others. Women, especially African-American women, turn on the "light" switch in your minds and put Mother Nature back on the course of harmony.

Men and women of today also have to understand that the media—from the news, the music we listen to, to what we see on television—play a big part on people's daily influences. The media mainly for providing information and entertainment through the freedom of self expression and creativity. Understand that we cannot imitate everything we hear and see. Just enjoy it, and/or use the information provided as positive motivation

THE CIVILIZED MARRIAGE

The civilized marriage is when a confluence between beings are connected with knowledge, wisdom, and understanding of a prosperous living for eternity. I used the word beings because being could mean existence or living creature. Some people are married to money, to one another, lifestyle, etc. Once you commit yourself to marriage, you made a promise to combine your everlasting essence in which a chance for divorce is slim to none. Before this can happen, we must have knowledge, wisdom, and understanding of ourselves. Know your strengths, know your weaknesses, and know what "nouns" that you will allow and not allow in your life.

Discuss as many great benefits and consequences that are possible with the connection of marriage. Then agree to unconditionally love and accept all the values and flaws that the being brings to the table. Stand firm on it and communicate clearly and honestly. Communication is the most important key to any type of relationship in order to keep it binding.

This is where the who, what, when, where, why, and how of your thinking process really comes into play. You might ask, "How do I communicate to money, a lifestyle, etc.?" This is that voice in your head that help directs your decision making, usually weighing out the options of benefits and consequences and determining whether or not you are robust enough to handle either. Changes are inevitable in marriage or any type of relationship, so discuss the "what-if" of possible occurrences, whether it would be good or unfitting change within your being(s). Then, you must decide if you are able to put up with the possible changes, compromise, or not accept that particular change. If a person is not willing to commit himself to a lifestyle of taking care of himself or his environment, what makes you think that anyone else will commit to him? Or if you don't know how to take care of yourself, how will you be able to take care of anyone else? Think about it for a moment. I have met men who said that when they get paid, "I just give my check to my wife and she gives me $20 and a pack of cigarettes for the week." I have met women who do not know how to cook a healthy meal. If there are some grey areas of your life that need attention, work on them individually or as a team.

Another important factor in keeping a marriage together is not allowing any outside interference into the relationship. Keep your personal business/issues between the two of you. Any influences should come from one another, God, or the power that be. Any outside support should come from a trusted, sound-minded individual, preferably someone professional, or from someone within your family tree who you trust and to whom you trust yourself around as well—as a fourth opinion. I've witnessed how a person's job can interfere and cause a marriage to split. Either it's because of working too much or not working enough. I have heard people say, "I can't make it without overtime."

There goes that "I can't" phrase again. Then, I will hear from the same person, "I'm tired of working seven days a week." So how do you find that happy medium? Focus on your health and make time for your family. Then contemplate a solid plan to turn the core of your hardships around, and then God or the powers that be will make sure everything else will fall into place and give birth to a harmonious lifestyle. Work smarter, not harder, and try to position yourselves into becoming your own boss. If any of these aspects are ignored, it simply fuels the WLL. More families will continue to split, which will lead to more unhealthy living beings falling victim to the war against themselves. Divorces decrease opportunities and increase all the chances for hardships of life that a lot of the lower class families are living in today, hardships such as poor health, teen pregnancies, incarcerations, lack of education, addictions, low income, crime, and many more. Go do some research. Don't just take my word. I challenge you to put your brain to work to attain some statistical facts for yourself. Numbers don't lie.

And as for the single individuals, you can't be emotionally or physically attaching yourself to a man or woman who has no ambition, nor has nothing beneficial to bring into your existence. You want someone who has your best interest at heart and expresses it through his or her words, and proves it with his or her actions. Women, how do you expect to find a respectable husband if you are in the club every weekend? Or, you can make time and money to get glamorous on the outside from head to toe, but lack in putting at least the same amount of attention to your inner self. Men, how do you expect to find a respectable woman when you spend the majority of your time playing video games all day every day? Or, you'll find yourself wasting time on nonessential things before you find time to invest into your well-being. All I'm saying is, get your priorities together first.

And for those of you with kids, the children are the future. Spend time and invest into them. If we take the time out right now, this WLL cycle can change for the better in just one generation. Married or not, don't be going around having babies when you're not up to par on taking care of yourself. Stand up to your responsibilities and stop waiting around and depending on the government or someone to come save you all the time. Focus on strength, stamina, patience, and resistance to worldly matters. Once you attained and worked on knowledge, wisdom, and understanding of your needs, your wants will become second nature in your life. You reap what you sow. I believe that people should enjoy life and the fruits of their labor; just make sure you are taking care of business and making healthy decisions before anything and strive to be as consistent as possible. What you reap will pay off tenfold.

WARNING: POSSIBLE INTERLOPING POSITIVES

This portion of the Willie Lynch Letter, he talked about the possibility of his system being destroyed. He pretty much provided the antidote to this sickening system. Lynch mentioned that if applied correctly, this system will last for at least 300 years or more, unless a phenomenon transpired and shifted the condition of the uncivilized male and female. So what does that tell you? It's time for the men and women to step it up and be more civil by working together to ensure a promising future for the next generation and the generations to come. Respecting one another more represent true humanitarianism—male respecting male, female respecting female, and male respecting female (and vice versa). Help one another, not pull one another down through violence, envy, and fear. Not anyone can succeed on his or her own; we all need help in some sort of way. And if you have kids, support their dreams and make sure they grow up with good manners and a vigorous, balanced mind, body, and soul. We are phenomenal people!

But it starts with bettering your health, strengthening the household, diverse higher learning, investing time into recreation, and future investments that will be everlasting for generations. We need more people to make an effort at being an asset to society by physically and financially contributing to their community. From signing up for a 5k walk/run to starting your own foundation; every endeavor is valuable in the strengthening of our environment. Correcting our well-being is the key to eliminating the WLL effect. Adults, we control the outcome of generations and the future. Ignorance must be erased from our lives and let great intentions reign upon Mother Nature, so that the essence of our existence shines as bright as the sun. The WLL is being kept alive by creating a multiplicity of illusions and attaching them to different levels of labor. This creates an entrapment of mental and physical slavery.

It may sound complex, but it's actually not. People just need to resist illusions of the irrelevant, have the serenity to recognize it, and not let it consume them. Illusions can vary. Read the definition of illusion and think about how it may be affecting you, the African-American societies, and mankind as a whole. Illusions are probably the seed of rhetorical devices that most people have no idea what it means or how to recognize it. It keeps one absentminded. I advise you to do some research on it.

To bring everything into its proper perspective in order for this turning point to head in the right direction, you have to learn about your history. Know your history, the counterpunches of the WLL that will annihilate its existence! Basically, learn as much as possible about whatever that existed. Learn about science. Learn about different creeds, cultures, religions, and lost civilizations. Mental history holds the reincarnated truth of the mind and the gateway to enlightenment. Déjà vu, karma, and the laws of nature are important factors of your essence battling for manifestation. Be more open minded and take in as much information as possible, and filter out and deflect the useless information. Remember, it has to be an event that causes a "shifting" of the male and female thinking process.

ABSOLUTE LANGUAGE

Controlling the language of the slaves is important for the continuation of the WLL effect. Lynch used the English language to manipulate the slaves for building economical success for the slave owners. Let's take a look at the word English and why this language was the best fit for the WLL. Do some research on the word English. To first understand English, you must have knowledge, wisdom, and understanding of it.

First, you must "know" that English is a collection and combination of various cultures. The dictionary is a good place to start. Read the full definition and all its meanings and directories. You will find that English derives from the word "angle." Read the full definition of the word angle and you will find that it has different definitions as well. The most important definition of the word angle that needs to be scrutinized is that it could mean an insincere personal motive, or the usage of schemes and tricks to get something. Now that you have become "wise" to the meaning of English, next will be to "understand" how the English language is used. Basically, the WLL controlled the language of the slaves by applying English to the minds of the slaves, so that they will be trapped within a spin of narrow-mindedness, while the oppressors had a "collection" of various outs within the communication. Like applying English to a ball that creates a spin in order to cause a change of direction, the same principle the WLL applies to the mind. This implementation misdirects your mind away from true intentions and your internal essence, which is good. We have to find ways to put a positive spin on things. Now, in relation to today's society, you have to be careful not only of what a person says to you, but how they say it. Understanding the "how" aspect opens the door of one's intentions and respect within human relations. What a person says and how a person says something can affect a person's progress in life.

A misinterpretation can cause a communication breakdown in relationships and cause a conversation to escalate into negative reactions. So we have to get back to the basic philosophy of learning about ourselves and how we think and speak, then mentally converse before we can have good conversations and understand someone's true intentions.

Place yourself in the other's person's shoes. Either it's one or two things he or she wants: to help or to hurt. Are you reliable, or are you a liability? You have to ask yourself, "Does this person care about and add value to my health, well-being, and economics? Or does this person take away from my health, well-being, and economics?" If you happen to get sucked into the WLL effect and get lost in conversations, ask questions to get a clear understanding and watch if a person backs up his words through his actions. There are powers in words that influence a person's present and future growth. This is the way to gaining absolute language understanding to determine the purity of one's existence, but most importantly, ending the effect of the WLL.

CONCLUSION
(P.S.A./PUBLIC SERVICE ANNOUNCEMENT)

According to FRAC (Food Research and Action Center) (2010), "Two-thirds of U.S. adults are overweight or obese (Flegal et al., 2012)" (paragraph 2). Out of the two-thirds, 82.1% are African-Americans. Loop21 reported that, "10 million people polled in a study conducted by the Census Bureau, African-Americans reported 11.5% rates of divorce, compared to 10% for whites, 7.8% for Latinos and 4.9% for Asians" (paragraph 3). *The NorthStar News & Analysis* (2012) pointed out that, "Black men had the highest incarceration rate of 3,059 per 100,000 U.S. black residents, which was nearly seven times higher than the incarceration rate for white men" (paragraph 7). The American Psychological Association (2012) confirmed that, "African-Americans and Latinos are more likely to attend high-poverty schools than Asian Americans and Caucasians" (National Center for Education Statistics, 2007, page 1).

The APA also reported that, "African-Americans are at higher risk for involuntary psychiatric commitment than any other racial group" (page 1). *USA Today* (2012) noted that, "The soaring national debt has reached a symbolic tipping point: It's now as big as the entire U.S. economy" (paragraph 1). And the list goes on.

Everyone, we have to do better. These are facts—numbers that need a change as we cross into a new age, determining if mankind will come together on one purpose and progress continuously, or keep living in this WLL labyrinth that has been plaguing our nation and the world for the past 300 years, which was expected to end on December 25, 2012. The WLL was designed to keep you distracted from finding enlightenment within your mind, body, and soul. What will the new age bring for mankind? It's up to all of us, the people who consciously and subconsciously support the WLL, and the people who are affected by it and want nothing more but to triumph over negativity. But being a critic is only half the battle. You must be able to provide sound solutions for any problem(s) that exist, prioritize, and execute the process. It takes a positive system to overcome a negative one. The best root system to use would be for each and every one of us to focus on getting healthy. We have to practice building an economically sound structure within our own mind and body before our nation and our world can prosper. Be consistent with ergonomics so you will know your self-worth and how to improve it. We have to stop being a liability by oppressing ourselves and spreading it around to our environment, our businesses. Think for a second. When an infant is born, what's one of the most important things required to sustain the infant's life?

Making sure he or she gets proper nutrition so he or she can grow and become strong. Somewhere in between birth and adulthood, we start making less healthy eating choices that affect our well-being. We have to get on track and eat better. Eating healthy and exercising regularly promotes not only a healthy body, but a healthy mind as well. Get to know who you are by being open minded, and explore other cultures and subjects of numerology, astrology, philosophy, etc. Be more diverse and creative by adding more art to our communities, like theatre, music, painting, etc. Create more programs for kids who are having difficulties in school. Add more recreational institutes instead of adding more liquor stores. Support one another and stop trying to pull one another down. Give mankind an opportunity to see how powerful and divine we can be. Anything is possible when we stay true to our essence.

Scientists have said that there is a possibility that the Earth's poles will flip off its axis on 12/21/12. Crossing into the new age can prove if the male and female can flip their state of mind to support mankind and the economics of the world, or suffer as a whole. For the past 300 hundred years, inevitable change has been manifesting with the destruction of the Willie Lynch Letter. Who would have thought that 300 years ago, African-Americans would have survived and exhibited such great success within this country, and the world for that matter? Phenomenal artists and humanitarians on various levels are increasing in numbers and getting stronger by the day. Who would have thought of powerful people such as Bill Cosby, Oprah, JFK, George Lopez, Bill Gates, Will Smith, Bruce Lee, Malcolm X, Martin Luther King, Jr., and many others would make such a magnificent impact on our world? People who promote life and provide opportunities…

Who would have thought that President Obama would be leading the United States of America on 12/21/12: four years ending an Age, and four years beginning a new one? We all are connected through our natural essence. We, as mankind, have to get physically and mentally fit, or die trying. Time wasn't created to be wasted. I encourage everyone to cultivate themselves more through reading, learning from one another, and physically being relevant at ascending to a level beyond our imagination in order to wane on pain and suffering. We do not live in a perfect world. If you just happen to not reach your goal, it's okay; pick yourself up, shake it off, and keep moving! Take heed. It's time for the world to wake up and make it happen! We are living in our last days of this age. This is the Rapture, the Resurrection, the Apocalypse, the Awakening, the key that has been right under the noses of mankind that will help free the minds of the lost. Let the trumpet of truth sound in your ear! This transformation into the new age is a turning point of maturity for mankind. Be the one to say, "I try to be a contributor to society in some form or fashion, and here's how. At the end of the day, when it comes to living a stress-free and healthy lifestyle, either you're going to spend a great portion of your life supporting and representing what's good or not. The choice is yours!

RESOURCES

American Psychological Association. (2012). "Ethnic and Racial Minorities and Socioeconomic Status. Retrieved from http://www.apa.org/pi/ses/resources/publications/factsheet-erm.aspx, Last Updated, 2012.

Byrne, Rhonda. *The Secret*. New York, NY/Hillsboro, Oregon: Atria Books/Beyond Words Publishing, 2006.

FRAC. (2010). "Overweight and Obesity in the U.S." Retrieved from http://frac.org/initiatives/hunger-and-obesity/obesity-in-the-us/, Last updated 2010.

LOOP21. (2012). "America Divorce Rates Drop Except for Black Couples." Retrieved from http://loop21.com/content/american-divorce-rates-drop-except-black-couples, Last updated, 2012.

Lowe, F., "Black Incarceration Rates Remain High, But Prison Population Drops Overall," *The NorthStar News & Analysis*, 2012. Retrieved from http://www.thenorthstarnews.com/Story/Black-Incarceration-Rates-Remain-High-but-Overall-Prison-Population-Drops, Last updated, 2012.

MedlinePlus (2012). "Heart risk still higher in blacks than whites." U.S. National Library of Medicine. Retrieved from http://www.nlm.nih.gov/medlineplus/news/fullstory_131075.html, Last updated November 7, 2012.

"The Willie Lynch Letter: The Making of a Slave!" *FinalCall.com News*, 2012. Retrieved from http://www.finalcall.com/artman/publish/Perspectives_1/Willie_Lynch_letter_The_
Making_of_a_Slave.shtml, Last updated 22nd May 2009.

Wolf, R., "U.S. Debt is Now Equal to Economy," *USA Today*, 2012. Retrieved from http://usatoday30.usatoday.com/news/washington/story/2012-01-08/debt-equals-economy/52460208/1, Last updated January 9, 2022.

www.ingramcontent.com/pod-product-compliance
Lightning Source LLC
Chambersburg PA
CBHW070524290526
45790CB00003B/1294